Table of Conten

Fan's Dictionary – Wolverhampton Wanderers F.C. Songbook

About This Book	3
A	5
B	10
C	14
D	19
E	24
F	29
G	33
H	37
I	39
J	49
K	53
L	57
M	59
N	68
O	74
P	77
R	79
S	82
T	93
U	99

W 101

Y 121

Over the years Wolverhampton Wanderers F.C. fans have created incredible atmospheres in football grounds and come up with some of the creative chants and songs. This book is a guide for these chants and songs written by the Wolverhampton Wanderers F.C. supporters.

From Those Were The Days, Everywhere We Go, North Bank Took Coventry, Falling in Love With You, Boys of The Black Country, Born Under a Wanderers Scarf, to songs dedicated to the various players and staff, the very best of the terrace chants, songs, and timeless classics, this book will delight and entertain in equal measure and honors every single Wolverhampton Wanderers F.C. fan who has ever sung in support for the team throughout its proud history.

All the songs and chants in this book are written and sang by the Wolverhampton Wanderers F.C. supporters during football matches, at pubs and bars or posted to message boards, they are not the thoughts or views of the authors.

WRITE TO US

We greatly value your opinion. We would love to hear your thoughts and recommendations about this book so we can improve! Write to us: fansdictionary@gmail.com

COPYRIGHT

Copyright © 2020 by Fan's Dictionary

The author have provided this book to you for your personal use only. Thank you for buying and for complying with copyright laws by not reproducing, scanning, or distributing any part of it in any form without permission.

ADAMA TRAORÉ

Adama Traoré,
Adama Traoré,
Adama Traoré...

ALEX MCLEISH

Cheer up Alex McLeish,
Oh what can it mean,
To a fat Scottish b**tard,
And a s*ite football team...

ALEX RAE

Follow, follow, follow,
There was only two minutes to go,
It was Alex Rae's goal,
That sent us out of control,
And sent Reading out the play-offs...

ALEX RAE 2

Alex Rae Alex Rae,
Alex Alex Rae,
He's got no hair but we don't care,
Alex Alex Rae...

ALL GONE QUIET OVER THERE

At's all gone quiet over there,
All gone quiet over there,
All gone quiet, all gone quiet,
It's all gone quiet over there,
And there and there and there and there and there...

ALL WE ARE SAYING

All we are saying is give us a goal,
All we are saying is give us a goal,
All we are saying is give us a goal...

AND IT'S WOLVERHAMPTON

And its Wolverhampton,
Wolverhampton Wanderers,
We're by far the greatest team,
The world has ever seen...

ANDY GRAY

He's here, he's there,
He's every-f***ing where,
Andy Gray, Andy Gray...

ANDY KEOGH

We love you Keogh,
Even though you're sh**e,
We love you Keogh,
Even though you're sh**e,
We love you Keogh because you really try hard...

ANDY KEOGH 2

He's blonde, he's sh*t,
He gets a game when no-one's fit,
Andy Keogh, Andy Keogh...

ANDY KEOGH 3

Keogh, Keogh, Keogh, Keogh...

ANDY KEOGH 4

Na na na na-na-na-na, na-na-na-na,
Keogh...

ANDY KEOGH 5

Oh Andy Keogh, you are the love of my life,
Oh Andy Keogh, I'd let you to s**g my wife,
Oh Andy Keogh,
I want long blonde hair too.

ARE YOU BAGGIES

Are you baggies, are you baggies,
Are you baggies in disguise,
Are you baggies in disguise...

ARE YOU WATCHING BBC

Are you watching, are you watching,
Are you watching BBC,
Are you watching BBC...

AWAY IN A MANGER

Away in a manger,
No crib for a bed,
The little Lord Jesus,
Looked up and he said,
We all hate West Brom,
We all hate West Brom...

BAGGIES BEST CLOTHES

Let's all go Tescos,
Where Baggies buy their best clothes,
Na naa naa na,
Na naa naa na...

BAGGIES NIL WANDERERS THREE

I'm gonna tell ya how it's gonna be,
Baggies nil and Wanderers three,
I'm gonna tell ya now who's gonna score,
Dougan two and Bernard Shaw,
Dougan two and Bernard Shaw.

BAKARY SAKO

Bakary, Bakary, Bakary, Bakary, Bakary,
Bakary,
Bakary Sako.

BARMY ARMY

Barmy Army,
Barmy Army,
Barmy Army...

BERTIE MEE SAID

Bertie Mee said to Bill Shankly,
Have you heard of the North Bank Highbury,
Shanks said no, I dont think so,
But I've heard of the Wanderers Boot Boys.

BEST TRIP

Don't want to go home,
Don't want to go hoooome,
This is the best trip I've ever been on.

BLACKPOOL ROCK

Suck his c*ck it's Blackpool rock,
Do-dah, do-dah…

BORN UNDER

I was born under a Wanderers scarf,
Do you know where hell is,
Hell is at West Brom (sh*t),
Heaven is at Molineux and that's where I'm from,
I was born under a Wanderers Scarf.

BOW LEGGED CHICKEN

I'm a bow legged chicken,
I'm a knock kneed hen,
I ain't had a w*nk since I don't know when,
I walk with a wiggle, and I talk with a squawk, killing the Albion boot boys.

BRING BACK OUR STEREO

Bring back our stereo, TV and video,
Bring back our stereo, TV and video,
Bring back our stereo, TV and video,
Bring back our stereo, TV and video...

BRUMMYS HAVE STAYED AT HOME

The Brummys have stayed at home,
Watched it on the tele,
The Brummys have stayed at home,
Watched it on the tele...

BUILD A BONFIRE

Build a bonfire,
Build a bonfire,
Put the Albion on the top,
Put the Villa in the middle,
And burn the f***ing lot.

CAN YOU HEAR

Can you hear the Scousers sing,
No, no,
Can you hear the Scousers sing,
No, no,
Can you hear the Scousers sing,
I can't hear a f**king thing.

CARL IKEME

Ikeme, in the middle of our goal,
Ikeme, in the middle of our goal,
Ikeme, in the middle of our goal...

CHAMPIONS LEAGUE YOU'RE HAVING A LAUGH

Champions League, you're 'avin a laugh,
Champions League, you're 'avin a laugh...

CHAMPIONSHIP YOU'RE HAVING A LAUGH

Championship, you're 'avin a laugh,
Championship, you're 'avin a laugh...

CHAMPIONY

Championy, championy, ole, ole, ole,
Championy, championy, ole, ole, ole,
Championy, championy, ole, ole, ole...

CHARGE IN A MINUTE

Charge in a minute,
We're gonna charge in a minute,
Charge in a minute,
We're gonna charge in a minute...

CHIM CHIMINEY

Chim chiminey,
Chim chiminey,
Chim chim cheroo,
We hate those b**tards in claret and blue.

CHIM CHIMINEY 2

Chim chiminey,
Chim chiminey,
Chim chim cheroo,
If you give it to Jota he'll score one for you.

CHRIS IWELUMO

What a friend we have in Jesus,
He's a saviour from afar,
What a friend we have in Jesus
And his name is Iwelumo.

CIRCUS IN THE TOWN

There is a circus in the town (in the town),
Martin O'Neil is a clown (is a clown),
Randy learner is a f**king t*at,
And the Villa are going down, going down.

COME ON WANDERERS

Come on Wanderers,
Come on Wanderers,
Come on Wanderers...

COME ON YOU WOLVES

Come on you Wolves,
Come on you Wolves,
Come on you Wolves....

CONOR COADY

They say he is a Scouser,
He's really Gold and Black,
His name is Conor Coady,
The leader of the pack,
This man is really magic,
He's Wanderers through and through,
He hates the f***ing Albion,
The Villa and the Blues,
(Allez, Allez, Allez)

DEAN RICHARDS

Deano, Deano, Deano, Deano...

DEAN SAUNDERS

Left your car at the airport,
You should have left your car at the airport.

DELIAH ONLY TAKES

Delilah only takes it, Delilah only takes it,
Delilah only takes it up the a*se,
Delilah only takes it up the a*se,

DEREK DOUGAN

Suuuuper, super Dougan
Suuuuper, super Dougan
Suuuuper, super Dougan
Super Derek Dougan.

DEREK DOUGAN 2

His name is Derek Dougan from Leicester he did come,
To play for Bill McGarrys men back in division one,
And if you come to Molineux you will hear us sing,
Wanderers are the greatest and Dougan is the King.

DIBBLE

We don't need no police protection,
We don't need no ground control.
Hey dibble, leave those kids alone...

DIOGO JOTA

It's Diogo, not Diego,
Makes me happy, makes me feel this way.

DIOGO JOTA 2

Diogooooo, Jota,
Running down the wing,
Jota, hear the Wanderers sing,
Jota, we're all going Gdańsk.

DIOGO JOTA 3

There's a star man,
Playing down the right,
His name's Diogo Jota and,
He's f**king dynamite.

DIOGO JOTA 4

Wake me up,
Before you go go,
Who needs Sako,
When you got Diogo.

DIRTY LEEDS

Dirty Leeds,
Scum,
Dirty Leeds,
Scum,
Dirty Leeds,
Scum...

DISGRACE TO THE PREMIER LEAGUE

Disgrace,
To the Premier League,
Disgrace,
To the Premier League,
Disgrace,
To the Premier League,
Disgrace,
To the Premier League...

EARLY BATH

Early bath, having a w**k,
Early bath, having a w**k,
Early bath, having a w**k,
Early bath, having a w**k...

EIEIEIO

EIEIEIO,
It's up the Football League we go,
And when we get promoted,
This is what we'll sing,
We are Wanderers, we are Wanderers,
And McCarthy is our king...

EMPTY SEATS

They're here, they're there,
They're every f*cking where,
Empty seats, empty seats...

EMPTY SEATS MY LORD

Empty Seats my lord,
Empty Seats,
Empty seats my lord,
Empty seats,
Oh lord empty seats...

EVERYWHERE WE GO

Everywhere we go,
People want to know,
Where the hell are you from,
We're from Wolverhampton,
Lovely Wolverhampton,
Colourful Wolverhampton.

Buy a corner shop now,
Sell a cheaper lager,
Tennants Extra 54p a can,
Banks's mild 42p a can...

..Tennants Super 68p a can,
Vimto for the right side.

Buy a taxi firm now,
Run a cheap Cortina,
With a nodding doggy 26p a mile,
With a furry dashboard 38p a mile,
Cortina supra 94p a mile,
A Datsun for the right side.

Buy a market stall now,
Sell a cheaper wrist watch,
Rolex International 34p a tick,
Roles supra 46p a tock,
Times delux £30,50,
Times from Bombay £4 only,
Big Ben for the right side.

Buy a take away shop,
Sell a cheaper poppadom,
Chicken Rangoon £1,40...

..Chicken Madrass £1,20,
Curry Sauce 32p a tub,
Beansprouts for the right side.

Buy a cheaper boat now,
Sail to sunny England,
Smuggle in Ranjit - on a forged passport,
With loads and loads of cocaine - hidden in a suitcase,
Ranjits got Aids now,
Transfusion for the right side.

Buy a terraced house now,
Send for all your relatives,
20 in the bathroom - 40 in the bedroom,
Buy som cheaper paint now,
Paint the outside orange - paint the inside purple,
A Palace for the right side...

...Signing on the dole now,
Claim for 30 children - 6£ a stinky,
Claim for many wives now,
And all the ones in Bombay,
Get a massive dole cheque - buy a lot of cheap gold,
Diamonds for the right side.

Buy a football club now,
Call it Wolverhampton,
Get promotion - in the first season,
Get relegated - sack the Bhattis,
Sack the Bhattis,
Find some new directors,
Wolves are back in business.

FA CUP WOLVES

Fa Cup,
Who gives a f**k,
We are Super Wolves,
And we are staying up...

FALLING IN LOVE WITH YOU

Take my hand,
Take my whole life too,
Cos I can't help,
Falling in love with you...

FAT AND SCOUSE

He's fat,
He's Scouse,
He'll rob you're f**king house,
The referee,
The referee.

FAVOURITE SONG

Your favourite song,
Is f**king s*ite,
Your favourite song,
Is f**king s*ite...

FIT TO REFEREE

You're not fit,
You're not fit,
You're not fit to referee,
You're not fit to referee...

FIVE OF YOU SINGING

5 of you singin',
There's only 5 of you singin',
5 of you singin',
There's only 5 of you singin'...

FOLLOW THE WANDERERS

We will follow the Wanderers over land and sea and water,
We will follow the Wanderers on to victory,
All together now...

FOOT AND MOUTH

You'll get it,
You'll get foot and mouth,
You'll get it,
You'll get foot and mouth,
Just like the scum,
Standing in the Holte End,
You'll get foot and mouth,
You'll get it...

FOOTBALL IN A LIBRARY

De de de,
Football in a library,
De de de,
Football in a library...

FREDDY EASTWOOD

Oh Freddy is a top lad,
He owns a caravan,
He'll tar up your front garden,
And then he'll charge your nan,
He scored against United,
Got booked against the s*ite,
And when he play's for Wanderers,
He'll score all f**king night...

GARETH BALE

Gareth Bale's got a f**king monkey's head,
F**king monkey's head,
F**king monkey's head...

GARY MEGSON

Cheer up Gary Megson,
Oh what could it be,
For a fat ginger b**tard,
With a sh*t football team.

GEORGE ELOKOBI

Der der der,
Georgey Elokobi,
Der der der,
Georgey Elokobi,
Der der der,
Georgey Elokobi...

GEORGE NDAH

George Ndah my lord,
George Ndah,
Oh lord George Ndah.

GET INTO 'EM

Get into 'em, f**k 'em up,
Get into 'em, f**k 'em up,
Get into 'em, f**k 'em up,
Get into 'em, f**k 'em up...

GIVE ME

Give me an W...W,
Give me an O...O,
...
What have you got,
We got the best team in the land,
We got the best team in the land...

GLORY GLORY WOLVERHAMPTON

Glory glory Wolverhampton,
Glory glory Wolverhampton,
Glory glory Wolverhampton,
And Wolves go marching on on on..

GO HOME

Go home,
You might aswell go home,
You might aswell go home,
You might aswell go home...

GOING DOWN

They're going down,
They're going down,
They're going,
The s*it are going down...

GOING UP

The s*it are going down and the Wolves are going up,
The Wolves are going up,
The Wolves are going up,
The s*it are going down and the Wolves are going up,
The Wolves are going up,
The Wolves are going up...

GRAND OLD TEAM

We're a grand old team to play for,
We're a grand old team to see,
And if you know your history,
It's enough to make your heart go ohohoh,
We don't care what the Albion say,
What the hell do we care,
For we only know, that there's gonna be a show, and the Wolves will be there er er.

HAVE YOU EATEN ALL YOUR MATES

Have you eaten,
Have you eaten,
Have you eaten all your mates,
Have you eaten all your mates...

HELDER COSTA

There's a star man playing on the right,
He's name is Helder Costa,
And f**king dynamite.

HELLO HELLO

Hello, hello,
We are the Wanderers boys,
Hello hello you'll tell by our noise,
We're up to our knees in Albion's blood,
We we are the Wanderers boys...

HERE WE GO

Here we go,
Here we go,
Here we go,
Kightly's better than Ronaldo,
Here we goooooo,
S***ing all over the scum.

HI HO WOLVERHAMPTON

Hi-Ho Wolverhampton,
Everywhere you go there's aggro,
I see your boots are shining,
And I'll make a fuss about The Wanderers.

HOW DO YOU WATCH THIS

How do you watch this,
How do you watch this,
How do you watch this every week...

I CAN RIDE A TRACTOR

I can't read and I can't write,
But it don't really matter,
I'm an Ipswich Town fan,
And I can ride a tractor...

I DO LIKE TO BE BESIDE THE SEASIDE

Oh I do like to be beside the seaside,
I do like to be beside the sea,
I do like to stroll along the prom prom prom,
Where the brass band play f**k of West Brom (and birmingham).

I HEAR THE SOUND

I hear the sound of distant bums,
Over there, over there,
And do they smell, like f***ing hell,
Over there, over there.

I LOVE TO GO WANDERING

I love to go a wandering,
Along the mountain track,
And when I go a wandering,
My knapsack on my back,
Up the Wolves, up The Wolves,
Up the Wolves, the Wolves.

I WANNA BE A WANDERERS RANGER

I wanna be a Wanderers Ranger,
I wanna live a life of danger,
I wanna beat Baggies every week,
I wanna chase 'em down the streets,
Here's to the girl who I like best,
Every night I suck her breasts,
S**g her standing, s**g her lying,
If she had wings, I'd s**g her flying,
Now she's dead, not forgotten,
Dig her up, s**g her rotten,
Ooooooooooh... Wanderers,
Ooooooooooh... Wanderers...

I WANNA GO HOME

I wanna go home, I wanna go home,
This is a s*it hole, I wanna go home...

IF YOU CAN'T TALK PROPER

If you can't talk proper shut your mouth,
If you can't talk proper shut your mouth,
If you can't talk proper,
If you can't talk proper,
If you can't talk proper shut your mouth...

IF YOU GO DOWN TO THE WOOD

If You go down to the wood today,
You'll hardly believe your eyes,
If you go down to the woods today,
You'll be in for a big surprise,
For Jeremy the sugar puffs bear,
Has bought some Dockers and cropped his hair,
Today's the day that Jeremy joined the,
Skinheads.

I'M FOREVER BLOWING BUBBLES

I'm forever blowing bubbles,
Pretty bubbles in the air,
They fly so high,
They touch the sky,
And like West Brom they fade and die.

Birmingham's always running,
Villa's running too,
We're the Super Wolves
And we're running after you.
The wanderers (clap) (clap) (clap),
The wanderers...

IMPOSSIBLE DREAM

To dream the impossible dream,
To fight the unbeatable foe,
To bear with unbearable sorrow,
To run where the brave dare not go,
To right the unrightable wrong,
To love pure and chaste from afar,
To try when your arms are too weary,
To reach the unreachable star.
This is my quest, to follow the Wolves,
No matter how hopeless,
No matter how far,
To fight for the Wolves,
Without question or pause,
To be willing to march into hell,
For the Molineux cause,
And I know if we'll only be true,
To this glorious quest,
We'll reach our unreachable goal,
To reach our unreachable goal.

IN THE ALBION SLUMS

In the Albion slums,
You search through the dustbin for something to eat,
You find a dead rat and think it's a treat,
In the Albion slums, in the Albion slums.

Your moms on the game and your dads in the nick,
You can't get a job cause you're so f**king thick,
In the Albion slums, in the Albion slums.

You p*ss on the pavement and sh*t in the bath,
You finger your nan and think it's a laugh,
In the Albion slums, in the Albion slums.

INCY IS A WOLVES FAN

Incy is a Wolves Fan,
Na na na na,
Incy is a Wolves Fan,
Na na na na...

IS THERE A FIRE DRILL

Is there a fire drill,
Is there a fire drill,
Is there a fire drill,
Is there a fire drill...

IS THIS A LIBRARY

Is this a library,
Is this a library,
Is this a library,
Is this a library...

ISAAC OKORONKWO

He sticks his left leg in, left leg out,
In out in out, he shakes it all about,
He does the Okowonko,
And he turns around,
That's what his all about,
Oh oh okowonko, Oh oh okowonko,
Oh oh okowonko,
Knees bent, arms stretched, ra ra ra...

IT'S CAMARA

When it misses the goal and lands in the North pole it's Camara,
And it's wide of the net it's a f**king good bet it's Camara,
When the balls in the sky and a mile too wide it's Camara,
With his slick orange boots but the f**ker can't shoot it's Camara...

JACK HAYWARD

Jack Hayward's barmy army,
Jack Hayward's barmy army,
Jack Hayward's barmy army,
Jack Hayward's barmy army...

JAMIE O'HARA

O'Hara Wooaaaahh, O'Hara Wooaahh,
He scored against the s*it,
His girlfriend's pretty fit,
O'Hara Wooaaaahh, O'Hara Wooaahh.

JARVIS AND KIGHTLY

Jarvis and Kightly, Jarvis and Kightly,
Runnin' down the wings,
Hear the South Bank sing,
Jarvis and Kightly...

JEFF SHI

Jeff Shi went to Saudi to buy a Lamborghini,
He came back with a striker, whose name is Bonatini,
He bought Diogo Jota, Ruben Neves too,
And got rid of Paul Lambert, 'cause he doesn't have a clue.

JIM MCCALLIOG

Jimmy, Jimmy Mac,
He plays in gold and black....

JINGLE BELLS

Jingle bells, Astle smells,
Ashman's got no hair,
Tony Brown is a clown and Suggett is a spare.

JOAO MOUTINHO

Oh Joao Moutinho, he loves a vino,
He came from Monaco, to Wanderers (to Wanderers),
He's 5 foot seven, he's football heaven,
So please don't take Moutinho away...

JODY CRADDOCK

He's here, he's there,
He's every f**king where,
Jody Craddock, Jody Craddock...

JODY CRADDOCK 2

There's only one Jody Craddock,
One Jody Craddock, one Jody Craddock,
He used to be s*ite,
But now he's alright,
Walking in a Craddock wonderland...

JOHN RICHARDS

Oh Johnny, oh Johnny,
You're the greatest in the land,
Oh Johnny, Johnny Richards,
You're the greatest in the land.

JONNY OTTO

Jonny Otto, Jonny Otto, Jonny Otto…

JONNY BOLY PATRICIO AND MOUTINHO

We've got Jonny du du du du du du,
Oh Willy Boly du du du du du du,
Rui Patricio,
And we've got Moutinho.

KARL HENRY

Karl Henry, whoa ah oh,
Karl Henry, whoa ah oh,
He comes from Ashmore Park,
He'll rob you in the dark.

KARL HENRY 2

Oooh Karl Henry,
He's neither here nor there,
Oooh Karl Henry,
He's f**king everywhere,
Oooh Ian Henry's,
Henry's gonna get you...

KEITH DOWNING

Psycho, Psycho, Psycho...

KENNY MILLER

Who put the ball in the Man U net,
Who put the ball in the Man U net,
Who put the ball in the Man U net,
Super Kenny Miller.

KEVIN DOYLE

Kevin Doyle is f**king magic,
Kevin Doyle is dynamite,
He'll score a sh*t load against West Brom,
Cause he knows they're f**king sh*te...

KEVIN DOYLE 2

One Kevin Doyle,
There's only one Kevin Doyle,
One Kevin Doyle,
There's only one Kevin Doyle...

KEVIN DOYLE 3

Oh Kevin Doyle, you are the love of my life,
Oh Kevin Doyle, I'd let you sh*g my wife,
Oh Kevin Doyle, we hate Albion too...

KEVIN DOYLE 4

Kevin Doyle is a wolf,
Is a wolf, is a wolf,
Kevin Doyle is a wolf,
He hates Baggies...

KEVIN FOLEY

Super, super Kev,
Super, super Kev,
Super, super Kev,
Super Kevin Foley...

KEVIN FOLEY 2

Foley,
He's Foley,
He's gold and black,
He plays right back he's Foley.

KNEES UP MOTHER BROWN

Knees up, Mother Brown,
Knees up, Mother Brown.
Under the table you must go,
Ee-i, ee-i, ee-i-oh,
If I catch you bending,
I'll saw your legs right off,
So, knees up, knees up,
Don't get the breeze up,
Knees up, Mother Brown,
Oh my, what a rotten song, sh*t,
What a rotten song, sh*t,
What a rotten singer too.

LEE HUGHES

Lee Hughes is a w*nker,
He plays for Albion,
His girlfriend is a prostitute,
Who comes from Birmingham,
She dances on the tables,
Her t*ts and a*se on show,
And if you wanna s*ag her,
It's twenty pence a go...

LEE HUGHES 2

You're supposed,
You're supposed,
You're supposed to be in jail,
You're supposed to be in jail.

LEEDS

Leeds, s*it, s*it, s*it...

LET HIM DIE

Let him die,
Let him die,
Let him die,
Let him die...

LET'S ALL HAVE A DISCO

Let's all have a disco,
Let's all have a disco,
Na na na na,
Na na na na.

LOYAL SUPPORTERS

Loyal Supporters, de de de de de,
Loyal Supporters, de de de de de,
Loyal Supporters, de de de de de...

MARCUS HAHNEMANN

Hahnemann do do do do do,
Hahnemann do do do do do,
Hahnemann do do do do do, do do do do do...

MARK RANKINE

Come on without, come on within,
You ain't seen nothing like the mighty Rankine.

MATT JARVIS

He runs down the left,
He runs down the right,
That's why Matt Jarvis makes Messi look s*ite.

MATT JARVIS 2

I saw my mate the other day,
He said to me he saw the white Pele,
So I asked who he is,
He goes by the name of Matt Jarvis,
Matt Jarvis, Matt Jarvis,
He goes by the name of Matt Jarvis,
Matt Jarvis, Matt Jarvis,
He goes by the name of Matt Jarvis...

MATT JARVIS 3

Jarvis for England, Jarvis for England...

MATT JARVIS 4

You are my Jarvis, my Mathew Jarvis,
You make me happy, when skies are gray,
Borja Valero was so much dearer,
So please don't take my Jarvis away...

MICHAEL KIGHTLY

De de de der Michael Kightly,
De de de der Michael Kightly...

MICHAEL KIGHTLY 2

He's here, he's there,
He's every bloodywhere,
Michael Kightly, Michael Kightly...

MICHAEL KIGHTLY 3

Oh Kightly's f**kin' magic,
He wears a magic hat,
And when he saw Molineux,
He said I fancy that,
He didn't sign for United,
Or Arsenal cos they're s**te,
He signed for Wolverhampton,
Cos they're f**king dynamite...

MICHAEL KIGHTLY 4

You are my Kightly,
My Michael Kightly,
You make me happy when skies are gray,
Oh Zoltan Gera was so much dearer,
Oh, please don't take my Kightly away...

MICK MCCARTHY

Mick Mccarthy's having a party, get your vodka and your charlie,
Mick Mccarthy's having a party, get your vodka and your charlie...

MICK MCCARTHY 2

We don't need no Phil Scolari,
We don't need Mourinho,
Hey, Moxey,
Leave our Mick alone.

MICK MCCARTHY 3

One leggg,
He's only got one leg,
He's only got one leggg...

MICK MCCARTHY'S BARMY ARMY

Everywhere we go, (Everywhere we go),
People want to know, (People want to know),
Who we are, (Who we are),
Where we come from, (Where we come from),
Shall we tell them, (Shall we tell them),
We're from Wolves,
Mighty mighty Wolves,
We're the army, the barmy barmy army,
Super Mick's barmy army,
Super Mick's barmy army,
Super Mick's barmy army...

MIKE STOWELL

We've got Mickey,
Mickey Stowell,
Mickey Stowell in our goal.

MIND THE GAP

Mind the gap, mind the gap Aston Villa,
Mind the gap, mind the gap I say,
Mind the gap, mind the gap Aston Villa,
It's getting bigger every f**king day.

MOLINEUX

We got the North Bank,
We dot the New Stand,
We got the South Bank Molineux.
We got the North Bank,
We dot the New Stand,
We got the South Bank Molineux.

MOURINHO'S RIGHT

Mourinho's right,
Your fans are sh*te,
Mourinho's right,
Your fans are sh*te...

MY GARDEN SHED

My garden shed,
(My garden shed),
Is bigger than this,
(Is bigger than this),
My garden shed is bigger than this,
It's got a door and a window,
My garden shed is bigger than this...

MY OLD MAN

My old man said be an Albion fan,
I said f**k off,
B**locks,
Off went the train the the South bank in it,
We took the Brummie road within a minute,
With wrenches and hammers,
Stanley knives and spanners,
We showed the b**tards how to fight...

NEIL COLLINS

There's only one Neil Collins,
One Neil Collins,
He used to be s*ite,
But now he's alrighte,
Walking in a Collins wonderland...

NEIL WARNOCK

Neil Warnock,
You're a w*nker,
You're a w*nker...

NENAD MILIJAS

Nenad Milijas oooooh,
Nenad Milijas oooooh,
He comes from Serbia,
And he'll f**kin murder ya...

NEVER WON

F**k all,
You're never won f**k all,
You're never won f**k all,
You're never won f**k all...

NO FANS

Sh*t ground, no fans,
Sh*t ground, no fans,
Sh*t ground, no fans,
Sh*t ground, no fans...

NO HISTORY

Sh*t club, no history,
Sh*t club, no history,
Sh*t club, no history...

NORTH BANK TOOK COVENTRY

At the turn of the century,
In the sky blue skies of Coventry,
A big golden banner and a big black bird,
And this was the song that Coventry heard.

10, 20, 30, 40, 50 or more,
Coventry supporters lying dead on the floor,
80 coppers died trying to end that spree,
The day the North Bank took Coventry.

Out on the pitch a hero arose,
Big John Tudor with a broken nose,
He came on the pitch looking for revenge,
But Duggie chopped him down,
Singing 'fioled again.

NORTH BANK SOUTH BANK

North Bank, (South Bank),
North Bank, (South Bank),
North Bank, (South Bank),
North Bank, (South Bank)...

NOT EVEN A CITY NOT EVEN A TOWN

Not even a city
Not even a town..
You play in a shed and Mowbrays a clown,
It's the West Brom, it's the West Brom,
You nans on the game,
Your dad is her p*mp,
Your sisters the same and you brothers her gimp,
It's the West Brom, it's the West Brom...

NOUHA DICKO

Nouha, Nouha, Nouha, Nouha, Nouha Nouha,
Nouha Dicko.

NUNO ESPIRITO SANTO

Nah, nah, na na na naaaaaa,
Na na naaaaaaa,
Nuno...

NUNO ESPIRITO SANTO 2

Nuno's the special one,
Nuno's the special one,
Nuno's the special one,
Nuno's the special one...

NUNO ESPIRITO SANTO 3

He's Nuno Nuno Nuno,
He'll take us to the Premier Premier Premier,
That's the way we like it like it like it,
In fact we f***ing love it love it love it...

NUNO ESPIRITO SANTO 4

Nuno had a dream,
To build a football team,
With Chinese owners and a wonderkid from Porto,
With five at the back,
And pace in attack,
We're Wolverhampton and we're on our way back...

ON THE PITCH

On the pitch,
On the pitch,
On the pitch,
On the pitch...

ONE MAN WENT TO WAR

One man went to war,
Went to war with Albion
One man and his baseball bat went to war with Albion.

Two men went to war,
Went to war with Albion,
Two men, one man and his baseball bat,
Went to war with Albion.

(Continue up to ten men)...

...Ten men went to war went to with Albion,
Ten men, nine men, eight men, seven men, six men, five men, four men, three men, two men, one man and his baseball bat went to war with Albion.

ONE NIL AND YOU F**KED IT UP

One nil and you f**ked it up,
One nil and you f**ked it up,
One nil and you f**ked it up,
One nil and you f**ked it up...

ONE NIL AND YOU STILL DON'T SING

One nil and you still don't sing,
One nil and you still don't sing,
One nil and you still don't sing,
One nil and you still don't sing.

ONE NIL TO THE DIRTY BOYS

One nil, to the dirty boys,
One nil, to the dirty boys,
One nil, to the dirty boys,
One nil, to the dirty boys...

ONE SONG

One song,
You've only got one song,
You've only got one song,
You've only got one song.

PARKES IS BETTER THAN YASHIN

Aye, aye, aye, aye,
Parkes is better than Yashin,
Ernie is better than Eusebio,
And we'll give Derby County a thrashin.

PETER CROUCH

S*ags for the money,
She only s*ags for the money,
S*ags for the money,
She only s*ags for the money...

PETER CROUCH 2

One Rodney Trotter,
There's only one Rodney Trotter,
One Rodney Trotter,
There's only one Rodney Trotter...

PETER CROUCH 3

Rodney you're a plonker,
Rodney you're a plonker,
Nanana, nananana...

PREMIER LEAGUE

Premier League is full of s*it,
Premier League is full of s*it,
Premier League is full of s*it...

PREMIER LEAGUE WE ARE COMING

Premier League, Premier League,
We are coming,
Premier League, Premier League I pray,
We are coming,
Premier League, Premier League,
We are coming,
We are coming at the end of May...

RATHER BE A DINGLE

I'd rather be a dingle than a c***,
Oh I'd rather be a dingle than a c***,
Oh I'd rather be a dingle,
Rather be a dingle,
Rather be a dingle than a c***...

RAUL JIMENEZ

There's something that the Wolves want you to know,
The best in the world and he comes from Mexico,
Our number nine,
Give him the ball and he'll score every time,
Si señor,
Give the ball to Raúl and he will score...

ROBBIE DENNISON

Oooh Robbie Robbie,
Robbie Robbie Robbie Robbie Dennison.

ROMAIN SAISS

Let's talk about Saïss baby,
He makes it look too easy,
He's got a pass success percentage rate of 83,
Let's talk about Saïss,
Let's talk about Saïss.

RONALD ZUBAR

He's big,
He's quick,
He's got a twelve inch d**k,
Zuuubarrrr Zuuubaarrrrr.

ROW ROW ROW YOUR BOAT

Row, row, row your boat,
Gently down the stream,
If you see The Albion,
Wipe him f*cking clean...

RUBEN NEVES

We've got Neves,
Ruben Neves,
I just don't think you understand,
He's Nuno Santos man,
He's better than Zidane,
We've got Ruben Neves...

SH*T ON THE ALBION

Sh*t on the Albion,
Sh*t on the Albion tonight,
Sh*t on the Albion,
Sh*t on the Albion tonight,
Everydody sh*t on the Albion,
Sh*t on the Albion tonight...

S*IT REFS

Sh*t refs,
We always get sh*t refs,
We always get sh*t refs,
We always get sh*t refs...

SAM VOKES

Sammy Vokes my Lord,
Sammy Vokes,
Oh oh Sammy Vokes...

SAM VOKES 2

Super, super sub,
Super, super sub
Super, super sub
Super Sam Vokes...

SAME OLD COCKNEYS

Same old Cockneys,
Always cheating,
Same old Cockneys,
Always cheating...

SAME OLD WANDERERS

Same old Wanderers,
Always winning,
Same old Wanderers,
Always winning...

SEOL KI-HYEON

Ki-Hyeun Seol (Seol)
He's gonna score 30 goals,
He's got the power to show,
He's indestructible,
Always believe in,
Ki-Hyeon Seol.

SEOL KI-HYEON 2

Seol, Seol where ever you maybe,
You eat dogs in your own country,
You could be worse you could be a scouse,
Eating rats in your council house...

SHALL WE KICK

Shall we kick, shall we kick,
Shall we kick f**k out of you,
Shall we kick f**k out of you...

S*IT MANCHESTER CITY

Sh*t Man City,
You're just a sh*t Man City,
Sh*t Man City,
You're just a sh*t Man City...

SHOES OFF IF YOU LOVE THE WOLVES

Shoes off if you love the Wolves,
Shoes off if you love the Wolves,
Shoes off if you love the Wolves,
Shoes off if you love the Wolves...

SIGN ON

Sign on, sign on,
With a pen in your hand,
Cos you'll never get a job,
You'll never get a job...

SING WHEN YOU'RE FARMING

Sing when you're farming,
You only sing when you're farming,
Sing when you're farming,
You only sing when you're farming...

SING YOUR HEARTS OUT FOR THE LADS

Sing your hearts out,
Sing your hearts out,
Sing your hearts out for the lads,
Sing your hearts out for the lads...

SIT DOWN AND BEHAVE YOURSELVES

Sit down and behave yourselves,
Sit down and behave yourselves,
Sit down and behave yourselves...

SIT DOWN SHUT UP

Sit down shut up,
Sit down shut up...

SOUTH BANK

South Bank, (clapping),
South Bank, (clapping)...

STALE SOLBAKKEN

Oh Stale Solbakken, la la la la la...

STAND UP IF YOU LOVE THE WOLVES

Stand up if you love the Wolves,
Stand up if you love the Wolves,
Stand up if you love the Wolves,
Stand up if you love the Wolves...

STAN BOWLES

Where's your wife gone,
Where's your wife gone,
Where's your wife gone Stanley Bowles...

STEARMAN AND MANCIENNE

Stearman and Mancienne,
Stearman and Mancienne,
Stearman and Mancienne,
Stearman and Mancienne...

STEVE BULL

We'll drink, a drink, a drink to Stevie the King,
The saviour of the Wanderer's Team,
Cos he's the greatest centre forward,
That the world has ever seen...

STEVE BULL 2

Hark now hear,
The south bank sing,
A new kings born today,
His name is Stevie Bull and he's better than
Andy Gray...

STEVE BULL 3

Oh, Stevie Bull's a tatter,
He wears the England cap,
He plays for Wolverhampton,
And he is a lovely chap,
He scores with is left foot,
He scores with his right,
And when we play the Albion,
He'll score all f***ing night.

STEVE BULL 4

Thank you very much for Stevie Bull,
Thank you very much,
Thank you very very much.

STEVEN MOUYOKOLO

He's clearing with his head,
He's clearing with his feet,
Gold and black defender to good to beat,
It's Mouyokolo, mouyokolo, mouyokolo,
mouyokolo, kolo.

SUPER MICK

Super, super Mick,
Super, super Mick,
Super, super Mick,
Super, Super Mick McCarthy...

SWEET MOLLY MALONE

In Dublin's fair city,
Where the girl's are so pretty,
I first set my eyes on sweet Molly Malone,
As she wheeled her wheelbarrow,
Through streets broad and narrow,
Singing, (clap, clap), The Wolves.

SYLVAN EBANKS-BLAKE

Na na na na na na nananana,
Sylvan Ebanks Blake,
Ebanks Blake,
Sylvan Ebanks Blake...

SYLVAN EBANKS-BLAKE 2

He's Big, he's Black,
He takes no f**king crap,
It's Ebanks Blakee, Ebanks Blakeee...

SYLVAN EBANKS-BLAKE 3

He hit the bouncer on the head, Sylvan, Sylvan,
The police they called it GBH, Sylvan, Sylvan,
He'll put the ball through someone's legs,
He'll turn around and shout nutmegs.
Ebanks Blake is Wanderers number 9,
Nanananana Ebanks Blake is Wanderers number 9.

SYLVAN EBANKS-BLAKE 4

He cost a million pounds last year Sylvan, Sylvan,
He'll score us 30 goals a year, Sylvan, Sylvan,
He scores them with his left or right,
Against the s*** he'll score all night,
Ebanks Blake is Wanderers number 9.

TAKE ME HOME

Take me home, Waterloo road,
To a place where I belong,
To the Molineux,
To see the Wanderers,
Take me home, Waterloo road...

TELL YOUR MA

Tell your ma your ma,
To put the Champagne on ice,
We've beaten the Albion twice.

TESCO CARRIER BAG

Always s**t on a Tesco carrier bag,
(Whistle, whistle),
Always s**t on a Tesco carrier bag,
(Whistle, whistle)...

THAT'S WHY YOUR GOIN DOWN

That's why your going down,
That's why your going down,
That's why your going down,
That's why your going down...

THE BAGGIES FAMILY

Your sister is your mother,
Your father is your brother,
They like to f**k each other,
The Baggies family...

THE BOYS OF THE BLACK COUNTRY

Fight, fight,
Where ever you may be,
We are the boys of the black country,
And we'll beat you all wherever you may be,
We are the boys of the black country...

THE HAWTHORNS IS FALLING DOWN

The Hawthorns is falling down,
Falling down,
Falling down,
The Hawtorns is falling down,
Poor old Baggies.

Build it up with Gold and Black,
Gold and Black,
Gold and Black,
Build it up with Gold and Black,
Poor old Baggies.

THE REF

The Referee's a w*nker,
The Referee's a w*nker,
The Referee's a w*nker,
The Referee's a w*nker...

THE SH*T OF BIRMINGHAM

You're the sh*t,
You're the sh*t,
You're the sh*t of Birmingham,
You're the sh*t of Birmingham...

THE SOUTH BANK

We're the South Bank,
We're the South Bank,
We're the South Bank Molineux...

THE WOLVES ARE STAYING UP

The Wolves are staying up and the sh*t are staying down,
The sh*t are staying down,
The sh*t are staying down...

THIS GROUND'S TOO BIG FOR YOU

This ground's too big for you,
This ground's too big for you,
This ground's too big for you,
This ground's too big for you...

THOSE WERE THE DAYS

Once upon a time there was a tavern,
Where we used to raise a glass or two, or three or four,
Where we used to while away the hours,
Thinking of the things we used to do,
Those were the days my friend,
We thought they'd never end,
We'd sing and dance for ever and a day,
We'd live the life we choose,
We'd fight and never lose,
For we're The Wolves, oh yes we are The Wolves...

TONY MOWBRAY

Cheer up Tony Mowbray,
Oh what can it mean,
To a sad Yorkshire b**tard,
And a sh*te football team...

TOP OF THE LEAGUE

Wanderers, Wanderers top of the league,
Wanderers top of the league...

TROPHY SPONSORED BY TEXACO

There's something that the Wolves want you to knowww,
We once won a trophy sponsored by Texacooo...

USELESS

De, de, de, de,
F**king useless,
De, de, de, de,
F**king useless...

WALTER ZENGA

Zenga, Zenga, Zenga,
Is taking us the Premier, Premier, Premier,
And that's the way we like it, we like it, we like it,
In fact we f**kin' love it, love it, love it...

WANDERERS BOYS ARE HERE

Wanderers boys we are here,
Wanderers boys we are here,
Wanderers boys we are here,
S*ag your women and drink your beer.

WARDYS NOSE

It's long, it's thick,
It's bigger than his d*ck,
Wardys nose, Wardys nose...

WASH YOUR HAIR

All you do is, all you do is,
All you do is wash your hair,
All you do is wash your hair...

WAYNE HENNESSEY

Hennessey, Hennessey, Hennessey...

WE ALL AGREE WOLVES ARE MAGIC

We all agree wolves are magic...

WE ALL HATE LEEDS

We all hate Leeds and Leeds and Leeds,
Leeds and Leeds and Leeds,
Leeds and Leeds and Leeds,
We all f*cking hate Leeds...

WE ALL HATE LEEDS SCUM

We all hate Leeds scum,
We all hate Leeds scum...

WE ALL HATE WEST BROM

Just last year, this is true,
The Sh*t went down, in Tesco white and blue,
They might go up, but until the date,
We'll sing this song that they f**king hate,
Championship, (W*nkers),
Championship, (W*nkers),
Championship, (W*nkers),
Championship, (W*nkers)...
...We all hate West Brom,
We all hate West Brom,
We all hate West Brom,
We all hate West Brom...

WE ALL LOVE WOLVES

We all love Wolves,
We all love Wolves,
We all love Wolves,
And we all love Wolves...

WE ARE THE PRIDE OF THE MIDLANDS

We are the pride of the Midlands,
The c*** of the North
We'll kill all the Scousers and Cockneys of course,
We'll kill them at home and we'll kill away,
We'll kill all the b**tards that get in our way.........cos,
Repeat...

WE ARE THE WANDERERS BOYS

Woh-oh, woh-oh, we are the Wanderers boys,
Woh-oh, woh-oh, we're here to make some noise,
And if you are an Albion fan surrender or you'll die,
Cos we all follow the Wanderers.

WE ARE TOP OF THE LEAGUE

We are top of the league,
I said we are top of the league,
We are top of the league,
I said we are top of the league...

WE ARE WOLVES WE ARE WOLVES

We are Wolves, we are Wolves, we are Wolves,
We are Wolves, we are Wolves, we are Wolves,
We are Wolves, we are Wolves, we are Wolves,
We are Wolves, we are Wolves...

WE BEAT THE S**T ONE-NIL

One-nil, we beat the s**t one-nil,
We beat the s**t one-nil,
We beat the s**t one-nil...

WE CAN SEE YOU SNEAKING OUT

We can see you sneaking out,
We can see you, we can see you,
We can see you sneaking out...

WE CAN'T TACKLE

We can't tackle, we can't tackle,
We can't tackle anymore,
We can't tackle anymore...

WE DON'T CARRY RAZORS

We don't carry razors, we don't carry lead,
We only carry hatchets to bury in your head,
We are Wolves supporters, fanatics everyone,
We hate Man United, Leeds and Everton.

WE GONNA WIN THE LEAGUE

We're gonna win the league,
We're gonna win the league,
Now you gotta believe us, now you gotta believe, now you gotta believe us,
We're gonna win the league...

WE HAD JOY

We had joy, we had fun,
We had West Brom on the run,
But the joy didn't last,
Cos the b***ards,
Ran too fast...

WE HATE

We hate Tottenham Hotspur,
We hate Chelsea too,
And we hate all the b**tards,
That play in white and blue.

WE HATE ALBION

We hate Albion,
Said we hate Albion (s*it),
We hate Albion,
Said we hate Albion (s*it)...

WE LOVE YOU WANDERERS

We love you Wanderers, we do,
We love you Wanderers, we do,
We love you Wanderers, we do,
Oh, Wanderers we love you...

WE NEVER WIN

We never win at home,
And we never win away,
We lost last week and we lost today,
But we don't give a f*ck,
Cos we're all p*ssed up, WWFC ok...

WE SHALL NOT BE MOVED

We shall not, we shall not be moved,
We shall not, we shall not be moved,
Top of the Championship,
We shall not be moved.

WE'LL NEVER DIE

We'll never die,
We'll never die,
We'll never die,
We'll never die,
Wanderers will never die,
We'll keep the gold flag flying high...

WE'LL NEVER PLAY YOU AGAIN

Again, we'll never play you again,
We'll never play you again,
We'll never play you again.

WE'LL SING ON OUR OWN

We'll sing on our own,
We'll sing on our own,
We are South Bank,
We'll sing on our own...

WE'RE COMING FOR YOU

We're coming for you,
West Bromwich Albion,
We're coming for you...

WE'RE JUST TOO GOOD FOR YOU

We're just too good for you,
We're just too good for you,
We're just too good for you,
We're just too good for you...

WE'RE ON THE MARCH

We're on the march with McCarthy's army,
We're all going to Wembley,
And we'll really shake 'em up,
When we win the FA Cup,
Cos Wolves are the greatest football team.

WE'RE THE BEST BEHAVED SUPPORTERS

We're the best behaved supporters when we win,
We're the best behaved supporters when we win,
We're the best behaved supporters,
Best behaved supporters,
Best behaved supporters when we win,
We're a right bunch of b***ards if we lose,
We're a right bunch of b***ards if we lose,
We're a right bunch of b***ards,
Right bunch of b***ards,
Right bunch of b***ards if we lose.

WE'VE GOT THE BEST TEAM

We've got the best team in the land,
We've got the best team in the land,
We've got the best team in the land,
We've got Peter knowles, scoring goals,
We've got Peter knowles, scoring goals,
We've got Peter knowles, scoring goals,
We've got the best team in the land.

WHAT A HOLE

What a f**king sh*t hole,
What a f**king sh*t hole,
What a f**king sh*t hole...

WHAT A WASTE

What a waste of money,
What a waste of money,
What a waste of money...

WHAT THE HELL WAS THAT

What the f**k,
What the f**k,
What the f**king hell was that,
What the f**king hell was that...

WHAT'S IT LIKE TO FOLLOW SH*T

What's it like to,
What's it like to,
What's it like to follow sh*t,
What's it like to follow sh*t...

WHAT'S IT LIKE TO SEE A CROWD

What's it like to,
What's it like to,
What's it like to see a crowd,
What's it like to see a crowd...

WHEN I WAS JUST A LITTLE BOY

When I was just a little boy,
I asked my mother what should I be,
Should I be Albion,
Should I be Wolves,
Here's what she said to me,
Wash your mouth out son,
And go get your fathers gun,
And shoot the Albion scum,
Shoot the Albion scum,
(We hate Albion, say we hate Albion)...

WHEN THE WOLVES GO MARCHING IN

Oh when the Wolves,
Go marching in,
Oh when the Wolves go marching in,
I wanna be in that number,
When the Wolves go marching in...

WHERE WERE YOU

Where were you, where were you,
Where were you when you were sh*t,
Where were you when you were sh*t...

WHERE'S THE W***ER

Where's the w**ker, where's the w**ker,
Where's the w**ker with the bell,
Where's the w**ker with the bell...

WHERE'S YOUR STATUE GONE

Where's your statue gone,
Where's your statue gone,
Where's your statue gone...

WHO ARE YA

Who are ya, who are ya, who are ya...

WHO DO WE APPRECIATE

Daisy daisy, give me your answer do,
I'm half crazy, all for the love of you,
It won't be a stylish marriage,
I can't afford a carriage,
But you'll look sweet,
Upon the seat, of a bicycle made for,
2 - 4 - 6 - 8,
Who do we appreciate,
W - O - L - V - E - S,
Wolves.

WHO THE F**K ARE MAN UTD

Who the f**k are Man Utd,
Who the f**k are Man Utd,
Who the f**k are Man Utd,
When the Wolves go marching on on on.

WHO'S THAT KNOCKING

Who's that knocking at the window,
Who's that knocking at the door,
It's Alan Ashman and his Mob selling Astle for a Bob,
Because they can't beat the Wanderers anymore.

WHO'S THE BAR STEWARD

Who's the bar steward,
Who's the bar steward,
Who's the bar steward in the black,
Who's the bar steward in the black...

WILL YOU COME TO MOLINEUX

Will you come, will you come,
Will you come to Molineux,
Will you come to Molineux...

WILL YOU EVER

Will you ever,
Will you ever,
Will you ever win the league,
Will you ever win the league...

WINGS OF A BLACK BIRD

If I had the wings of a black bird,
If I has the a*se of a crow,
I'd fly over West Bromwich Albion,
And sh*t on the b**tards below...

WIPE MY A*SE

You're not fit to,
You're not fit to,
You're not fit to wipe my a*se,
You're not fit to wipe my a*se...

WOLVES ARE GOING UP

Wolves are going up,
We're going up,
We're going,
Wolves are going up...

WOLVES TILL I DIE

Wolves till I die,
I'm Wolves till I die,
I know I am,
I'm sure I am,
I'm Wolves till I die.

WORST SUPPORT

Worst support,
Worst support,
Worst support we've ever seen,
Worst support we've ever seen

YAM YAM

Yam Yam Yam Yam youth,
Yam Yam Yam Yam youth...

YAM YAM

Oh oo Yam Yam army,
Oh oo Yam Yam army,
Oh oo Yam Yam army,
We are the Wolvessss...

YELLOW SUBMARINE

In the town where I was born lived a man with a dream,
And he told us of his life in a yellow submarine,
We all live in a yellow submarine, yellow submarine, yellow submarine,
The Wolves...

YOU ARE MY WANDERERS

You are my Wanderers,
My only Wanderers,
You make me happy, when sky's are grey,
You'll never know,
How much I love you,
Please don't take my Wanderers away.

YOU KNOW YOU ARE

You're s*it, and you know you are,
You're s*it, and you know you are,
You're s*it, and you know you are,
You're s*it, and you know you are...

YOU'LL NEVER REACH THE STATION

You'll never reach the station,
You'll never reach the station...

YOU'LL NEVER TAKE THE DONKEY

You'll never take the donkey,
You'll never take the donkey,
You'll never take the donkey,
You'll never take the donkey...

YOUR SONGS

Your songs,
We'll sing your songs for you,
We'll sing your songs for you,
We'll sing your songs for you...

YOUR SUPPORT

Your support,
Your support,
Your support is f**king sh*t,
Your support is f**king sh*t...

YOU'RE NOT FAMOUS ANYMORE

You're not famous,
You're not famous,
You're not famous anymore,
You're not famous anymore...

YOU'RE NOT GONNA STOP US

You're not gonna stop us,
You're not gonna stop us,
You're not gonna stop us,
We're going on the pitch...

YOU'RE NOT SINGING ANYMORE

You're not singing,
You're not singing,
You're not singing anymore,
You're not singing anymore...

YOU'RE NOT VERY GOOD

You're not very good,
You're not very good,
You're not very, you're not very,
You're not very good,
Sh*t...

YOU'RE THE BRUM

You're the Brum,
You're the Brum,
You're the Brum of Merseyside,
You're the Brum of Merseyside...

YOU'RE TOO FAT TO REFEREE

You're too fat,
You're too fat,
You're too fat to referee,
You're too fat to referee...

Made in the USA
Middletown, DE
28 October 2025